The Hole

Robert Swindells

Illustrated by
Tony Morris

OXFORD
UNIVERSITY PRESS

Hi. I'm Gaz, and I've got a story to tell. A true story. It's called The Hole. Sounds daft I know, but it isn't. It's a horror story where something's lurking, waiting.

One night there's this wild storm.
Thunder and lightning. Wind and
rain. The rain hits my window and
keeps me awake. Next morning
everything's soaked outside.

At school, the playing field is like a swamp. But me and my mates still want a game of footie.

At morning break, we go to the field. Miss Rose is on duty.

She says, "That field's like a swamp. Don't get all messy."

"No, Miss," we say, but we don't care if we do get messy.

I pick my team, Robbo picks his. We're about to kick off when Robbo says, "Hey, look at this."

I look. In the middle of the pitch is a
hole. It looks deep. I go as close as I dare.
It's black down there and I can't see the
bottom.

"Chuck something in," says Robbo. Everybody says, "Yes, chuck something in, Gaz." I pick up a lump of mud. When I drop it in the hole, I count.

"One, two, three…"

I count to seven, then we hear a splash. It's sort of echoey. It makes me shiver.

"Wow," says Robbo. "That's deep."

I nod. "Go and get Miss Rose, Robbo. I'll keep everyone back."

Robbo runs off. The other lads are creeping closer to the hole.

"Stay back," I yell. "It's not safe." I look across the field. "Hurry up, Miss," I whisper.

"Miss!" says Robbo to Miss Rose. "We found a hole with water in it!"

"Yes, well," she says. "Don't paddle in it and get your shoes dirty."

She thinks he means a little hole, see? A mud hole with a puddle. She turns away, drinking her cup of tea.

"No, Miss," says Robbo. "It's not just a puddle. It's really deep."

Miss Rose turns. "Well, then, stay out of it," she says.

Robbo starts to worry. He says, "Gaz chucked a lump of mud in, Miss. He counted seven before the splash."

The teacher gapes. "What?" He's got her attention now. "Are you winding me up, Robert South?"

"No Miss, it was seven. Then this splash, sort of echoey."

Miss Rose drops her tea.

Robbo's still talking, but she's running towards us. I'm glad, because the boys are creeping closer again. I act angry but they take no notice.

And just when I think it's over, Colin decides to jump over the hole.

He's not on my team, by the way. I wouldn't pick him. He's a nut. As Miss Rose comes puffing, he takes his run-up and leaps. Except there's no leap because I grab the hood of his jacket. Then the ground gives way under him.

It crumbles and falls into the hole. This time nobody counts, but we all hear the splash. That horrible, echoey splash.

Colin dangles by his hood, weeping with terror.

I'm flat on the grass, holding onto his hood. I nearly have to let go. Very nearly, but then Miss Rose arrives. Together, we pull him clear. Then the Head comes and takes charge. I'm glad, I'm fed up with the hole.

The rest of break is cancelled. Men
come with a truck. They put a fence
round the hole. By lunchtime, they've
fenced off the whole field. It's out of
bounds. There's just the tiny playground
left. We can't play footie there.

Later, we find out there used to be a coalmine. Way back, in the nineteenth century. The mine wasn't on any plans. When the coal ran out they laid boards across the hole.

As years went by, everyone forgot. Grass grew over the boards.

Nobody remembered there was once a mine. They built a school, with a deep mineshaft under the field. And nobody knew the boards were rotting.

Kids ran across them, jumped on
them. At any moment, the boards could
have broken and they would have fallen
down the mine.

They didn't know the mine was
flooded. Kids would have fallen into the
cold, dark water. The Hole lay hidden,
waiting to drown some kid.

It was like a horror story. Something dark and cold and lurking. Waiting. But it was a storm that made the boards collapse, not a kid. Sheer luck.

Goes to show you never know. And that's a poem.